The Illustrated
CAT

Women's Rights – A Meeting, 1885
William Henry Hamilton Trood (1860-1899)

The Illustrated
CAT

Tom Howard

CHARTWELL
BOOKS, INC.

Published by
Chartwell Books, Inc.
A Division of Book Sales, Inc.
Raritan Center
114 Northfield Avenue
Edison, NJ 08818
USA

ISBN 0-7858-0179-0

Printed in Italy

FRONT COVER
Marmalade Cat
by Joan Freestone (contemporary artist)

BACK COVER
Cats
by Julius Adam (1826-74)

RIGHT
Kittens at a Banquet
by Louis Eugene Lambert (1825-1900)

Contents

Introduction

The cat is so elegant and sensuous that it is an obvious subject for the artist. However, although the beauty of cats has been recorded in many paintings and sculptures, its image has been used more as a symbol than as a subject in its own right. At one extreme, this symbol personifies the forces of evil, at the other, the essence of security, home and comfort.

This book traces both that range of cat portraiture and the history of the cat and its relationship with people which produced such a variety of artistic representations. It looks back to the origins of the domestic cat and its first association with people in ancient Egypt, where it was associated with the gods, through periods when it was rejected and persecuted, to its present popularity as a favoured pet.

Why does the cat have such a particular place in our affections? A kitten has the wide-eyed appeal of all young animals, and the domesticated cat will often retain a kittenish playfulness through to old age. It is less demanding than a dog – clean by nature and with no need to be taken out for toilet trips or to drag its owner for long hikes pulling on a leash. It responds lavishly to attention with a reassuring purr. It demands less space and less food than larger animals and almost never bites the postman. Its soft fur and warm body are comforting to touch; stroking it creates a therapeutic calm. Not the least of its appeal is its appearance: most cats are elegant, often beautiful – and even a battle-scarred tom moves with sinuous grace.

Nevertheless, there is more to this decorative, comfortable companion in our homes. However domesticated it appears, curled asleep on a favourite chair, it retains its essentially wild nature and independence. Unlike the dog, whose domestication goes back much further into the mists of prehistory and which has been bred in a huge variety of forms and sizes to carry out specific tasks or satisfy human foibles, the cat, to all intents and purposes, remains unchanged. Appearance seems to deny that the Afghan and the Pug can really both be the same kind of animal, but all cats are clearly cats. Indeed, their similarity to other members of the cat family – tiger, cheetah, caracal, even the lion and the lynx – is still apparent. Human interference has begun to change the line of a nose, the length of fur and to develop colours and patterns that would have little chance of surviving in the competitive natural world, but the cat remains the quintessential cat. It is a creature of instinct and the world of tooth and claw is never far away, however soft and placid its appearance may be. In a very real sense, the cat remains 'the tiger on the hearth'.

The domestic cat tends to live by exploitation of a comfortable human home, and many a cat unhappy with its lot will desert a bad home if it can find a better. Often in the past – and even now in many countries – the cat is tolerated as a rodent- catcher, rather than encouraged as a pet. Sometimes it was actively persecuted and it may still be the victim of human cruelty. The pictorial record shows all aspects of the cat-human confrontation, as well as the elegant portrait and the sentimental scene. For over three thousand years artists have recorded the changing nature of that human-cat relationship. Its ambiguity, along with the charm and character of cats, is reflected in the pictures collected here.

Old Mr. Tombs
(after George Orwell: *A Clergyman's
Daughter*) by contemporary artist Ditz.
One of the parishioners in Orwell's first
novel, Mr. Tombs is a retired bookseller
who lies in bed all day under a fur rug
composed of 24 living cats because he
'found they kept him warm'.

7

The Cats of Bast

It is almost certain that the cat was first domesticated in Ancient Egypt. Cat bones have been found in excavations of 6,700 BC Jericho and at some even earlier prehistoric sites. However, there is nothing to suggest that these were domestic animals. In Egypt the mummified remains of thousands of cats have survived: animals that appear to be of the domestic type and of the wildcat from which it is most likely to have developed.

The domestic cat belongs to the species *Felis sylvestris* , the various geographical forms of which differ sufficiently for them to be classed as subspecies. The Scottish Wildcat, *Felis sylvestris grampia*, looks very like a modern household tabby. This wildcat might seem the most likely ancestor of our pets, but this subspecies and the closely related north European races have proved almost impossible to domesticate. The African Wildcat, *Felis sylvestris lybica*, is more amenable to sharing its life with people and it is this cat, with a coat variously striped, spotted or unmarked, that is found among the domestic mummies, together with a few examples of the Jungle Cat, *Felis chaus*. There is not yet proof that the domestic cat developed from the African Wildcat, but, with the technique of genetic fingerprinting, samples of ancient DNA may soon supply positive evidence.

How did domestication happen? Did the opportunist cat find human settlements a good hunting ground, with plenty of prey in the rodents attracted by Egyptian grainstores? Were they drawn there by scavenging opportunities? Or were cats or kittens captured and raised in captivity until they became used to humans? Answers can be only conjecture. The earliest known

The Cat Ra from the papyrus of Hunefer, dating from about 1300 BC.
Ancient Egyptian gods took many forms, and a cat was the form given to the sun god, Ra, at night, when his eyes held the sun's rays during darkness. In this shape, too, he was thought to battle with the serpent form of Apep (or Apophis), god of chaos and darkness. Each morning the snake was slain, but came to life again to create another night. During a solar eclipse the Great Cat's victory was in doubt . To encourage him in his struggle, Egyptians shook a rattle-like instrument called the sistrum, which was associated with the goddess Bast and often decorated with a cat figure or design.

representations of a cat are amulets and charms from the third millennium BC, when cats may already have had some role in Egyptian religion. Some of the Egyptian gods were seen in lion form or lion-headed. Later, some of the same gods or others developed from them appear with cats' heads. We know that sacred animals were kept in Egyptian temples – could the cat first have been a token temple animal, captured to represent its larger relation?

About 2,400 BC the worship of the sun god Ra became the state religion, centred on Heliopolis. The sun's heat was seen as coming from his eyes, which were represented by two goddesses. Sekhmet was the savage heat of the sun that burned the desert, Bastet was the gentler warmth that nurtured crops and life. Bastet was

later shown either as lion- or cat-headed and gained other attributes.

Bastet (or Pasht, or Bast as she became widely known) became increasingly associated with the cat. She became the patroness of those skilled in handcrafts, a source of fertility, associated with enjoyable things – music, dance and sex. Her cult centre was at Bubastis (the house of Bast), at the head of the Nile delta. Here the pharaohs Cheops and Chephren, who had built the Sphinx, erected a temple to the lion goddess. Later she was also worshipped there as a small cat, and temple cats were kept and tended by the priests. They were probably carefully watched to see if their behaviour conveyed any message from the goddess. Care of the sacred animals was an honour passed down from father to son among the priests.

Bast was not a major deity originally but, when Bubastis became the capital of Egypt under a new Libyan ruler in 945 BC, she became a national goddess worshipped throughout the land. At her annual festival thousands would arrive by boat, singing, dancing and indulging in ribaldry on the way to take part in an orgy of drinking and love-making.

By this time the cat had long been well-established in Egyptian homes and much loved by its owners. Paintings dating from about 500 years earlier, especially a group in the tombs of the Valley of the Nobles at Thebes, show domestic scenes with cats; others are of hunters out in the marshes of the delta in which cats appear. One of these reddish-coated, spotted or tabby cats is clearly collared with a lead attached, another is eating fish. One painted in the tomb of a sculptor, Ipuy, wears a silver ring in its ear while a kitten in the same painting plays on the sculptor's lap.

In the hunting scenes, cats are seen stalking wildfowl through the papyrus leaves or waiting for a bird to be struck down by the throwing-sticks that fly overhead. In a famous painting from the tomb of Nebuman at Thebes a cat, balanced precariously on a papyrus stalk, appears to have caught

A figure of the the goddess Bast in her cat-headed form, flanked by kittens. *In her right hand is a sistrum, which was shaken to emphasize the rhythmical beat of music. Like the goddess, it is particularly associated with sexuality, for its shaking sounded the rhythm of love-making. The Greek historian and travel writer Herodotus described Bast's great temple at Bubastis as one of the finest in Egypt, surrounded by a moat and shaded by trees, its walls decorated with figures twice life-size and with an inner grove of trees around the sanctuary containing the statue of the goddess.*

a duck by the wing in its teeth and to have grasped birds with both front and back paws. This is often taken as evidence that the ancient Egyptians taught cats to retrieve. They are known to have been skilled in training animals, and certainly many pet cats enjoy playing retrieval games if introduced to them when young – and Turkish cats around Lake Van and others living on the eastern Mediterranean coasts are sometimes seen to swim. However, despite its lifelike detail, this is not a realistic picture. The plentiful catch of both the cat and Nebuman, the way in which his wife is dressed and the abundance of fish and fowl reflect the hieroglyphs accompanying the image, which refers to pleasure and good things. The cat is a symbol of the enjoyment of plenty and sensuous pleasure that Nebuman and his wife hope to have in their afterlife. The domestic pictures, too, may carry a symbolic overtone, for the cat is most frequently placed beneath a chair on which the deceased's wife is sitting. Remember that Bast was the goddess of fertility and pleasure.

Whatever their symbolism, these pictures show that the cat was an established part of the Egyptian domestic scene, and cats became increasingly loved and venerated. Many animals were sacred to the Egyptians, but the cat was especially so. When Persian invaders advanced into the city of Pelusium in the mid-sixth century BC, their leader ordered them each to carry a cat before him. The defending Egyptians made no attempt to fight them and surrendered their city for fear of the cats' being harmed. The Greek historian Diodorus Siculus reports an incident involving a Roman diplomat in Ptolomaic times who accidentally killed a cat. He was nearly stoned to death by local people before he was rescued and got away with only paying a fine.

When a cat died the whole household would go into mourning, one sign of which was to shave off the eyebrows. The cat would probably then be mummified and taken to a

temple. Mummification was not so elaborate as for a pharaoh. Kittens were often just dipped in chemicals before being wrapped in bandages, but if owners could afford it, more care was taken with adult cats. Often they were housed in elaborate mummy cases or coffins of pottery, wood or metal. Another Greek writer, Herodotus, thought that all dead cats were taken to Bubastis and the embalming carried out there before the mummies were placed in the temple repositories. However, there are cat cemeteries associated with a number of temples, including the Bubastion at Saquarra and the temple of Pakhet, another cat goddess – or perhaps an avatar of Bast – at Beni Hassan on the middle reaches of the Nile.

Probably not all cats were mummified. At Bubastis itself excavations revealed great pits of burned remains with meagre evidence of mummy coverings or cases. Burned remains have been found elsewhere, too. Perhaps cremation was an alternative. Nevertheless, thousand of mummies have been found lining the tunnels of great necropolises which are sometimes shared with other sacred animals.

When Egyptians sought the goddess's favour they would make an offering at the shrine that would be used to purchase fish to feed the temple cats. Votive figures might also be presented, and the mummified cats themselves were probably considered a form of votive offering. Perhaps there was a trade in mummies for people who were visiting the shrine on occasions when they had no cat of their own to mourn. This might explain the wrappings that contain oddments of bone from other animals which have been presented as though they were cats. There could have been deliberate faking for commercial reasons. There are also cats which appear to have had their necks deliberately broken. This does not necessarily imply secret cat murders – there is also the possibility that there was an element of ritual killing, perhaps by priests of the temple, making more mummies available.

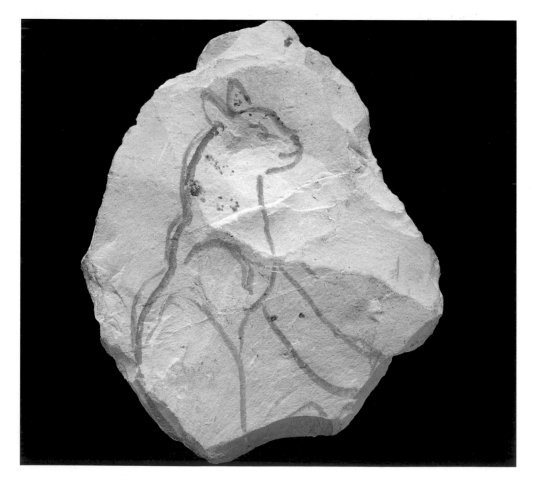

Part of a wall painting from the Tomb of Kenro, dating from the reign of Rameses II (1292-1225 B.C.) the cat beneath the chair of the deceased's wife Mutemuia wears a collar and is gnawing a bone. The various cats seen in such paintings shown under chairs are strong evidence that the cat was well established as a domestic pet in Egyptian houses at the time that they were painted. However, when positioned beneath the figure of a deceased man's wife, they may also have a significance as symbols of continuing sensuality and conjugal delight in the after-life.

ABOVE

A mural from the tomb of the sculptor Nebuman shows him wildfowling with his wife in the marshes of the Nile delta. His weapon is the throwing-stick which strikes the bird in the air. Is the cat, with its hold on three birds, a trained retriever, just being used to flush out the birds or used only symbolically as a promise of plenty, good hunting and fertility in the next world?

RIGHT

A bronze case which contained the mummified body of a cat. As well as being decorated with a seated cat, it is engraved with a prayer to the goddess Bast.

A cat mummy dating from the Late Period (664-332 BC) has been intricately wrapped in bands of linen, the head finished with a coat of stucco painted with stylized features. In mummification the internal organs were removed, often to be replaced by a sand filling. The body was dehydrated and preserved by rubbing in a naturally occurring mixture of sodium bicarbonate and sodium carbonate, called natron. The animal was then placed in a suitable posture, wound in a linen sheet and closely bandaged. A further cloth or papyrus covering might be decorated with paint or appliqué to suggest fur and features before the animal was placed in an outer case.

ABOVE
This fine bronze votive figure of a cat from the Saite period, c. 600 BC is known as the Gayer-Anderson cat, from the names of the donors who gave it to the British Museum. Egyptian paintings and sculptures show several cats wearing earrings or neck ornaments and, as with some diamanté-collared pets of today, Egyptians may sometimes have bedecked their household cats with jewellery. The ornamentation here is symbolic. This cat wears the protective Eye of Wadjet around her neck, on her chest is a winged scarab carrying the sun disc and on her head a scarab. Egyptians probably identified forehead tabby markings with this beetle sacred to the god Ra.

The spread of the cat

It was forbidden to take cats out of Egypt, but that did not prevent its happening, especially after Egypt became a Roman province following the defeat of Cleopatra in 30 BC. Some slipped out with Phoenician traders and were probably taken to the eastern Mediterranean and along the North African coast to Carthage and other places on their trading routes. The Minoans of Crete had close contacts with Egypt, and a terracotta head and some paintings of cats have been found there. However, it is from the sixth century BC that cats begin to appear in Greek art and bones are found in excavations which suggest domestication.

The Greeks do not seem to have rated cats very highly. Writers report on them as part of the Egyptian scene and even joke about the Egyptian attitude towards them. They are mentioned in Aesop's fables (if those particular stories are not later interpolations), but the Greeks seem to have relied more on the mongoose or some kind of ferret for their rodent control. Cats appear on coins, on some painted vases and in carvings. One carved relief shows young men with a cat and dog held on leashes while they size each other up, although the round ears on the 'cat' suggest that it is some other kind of animal. A Sicilian poet writing of the cat's love of comfort indicates that, by the third century, the cat was an established pet in the Greek colonies there.

In ancient times the house mouse and the rat were not endemic to Europe as they are today. Both spread outwards from the Middle East as human settlements and towns developed, or invaded merchant ships – the great influx of the brown rat did not come until the Crusades. Perhaps this is why no emphasis is placed on the cat as a rat-catcher.

ABOVE
A funerary stele, found on Salamis and now in Athens, commemorates a young man who died in the fifth century BC. It shows him with his boy slave, gesturing towards a bird cage and with a cat (now damaged) seated on a pedestal – evidence that domestic cats were known in Greece by then.

LEFT
A Roman stele from a cemetery in Gaul shows a dead child holding a cat, which must surely be a favourite pet. As the Roman legions brought Imperial power through Gaul and Britain, the cat followed the spread of Empire.

ABOVE
A relief on a statue base found in Athens shows youths introducing a dog and a cat, both collared and on leads. The dog appears to be making a typical 'play bow', inviting a game, but the cat is not so confident!

Nevertheless, sailors on the trading routes must have been glad to have one aboard and that is one way in which it probably spread. Indeed, geneticist Neil Todd showed that the distribution of black cats matches Phoenician trading routes and that of the blotched tabby later followed British trade routes and colonization.

At first, wealthy Romans probably welcomed the cat as an exotic pet, adopting it, like other Egyptian things such as the cult of Isis, more as a matter of fashion than for any practical reasons. However, in a book on agriculture a Roman of the Imperial period, Palladius, recommends it to protect gardens from moles and mice and, in post-Roman times, it became highly valued for its role in rodent control.

ABOVE
A mosaic from Pompeii, buried by the eruption of Vesuvius in AD 79, is almost identical to a Roman mosaic dating from the following century. This suggests that both may be based on some widely known painting, although they could simply result from keen observation, as the cat holds the bird ready to deliver the killing bite on the nape of the neck.

Good Luck — Bad Luck

By classical times the Egyptian cat goddess Bastet, like the Greek goddess Artemis and the Roman Diana, was associated not only with fertility, but with the moon and virginity – both the celebration of sexuality and its containment. To most people these would have been considered regional forms of the same deity, just as many Christians would later celebrate the Virgin Mary through devotion at a local shrine. It was natural, therefore, that the cat should become associated with the equivalent goddess in other religions. This was particularly appropriate in the case of the huntress Artemis/Diana.

In Northern Europe cats were also associated with the Teutonic goddess Freyja (after whom the fifth day of the week is named in English), another goddess of wealth and fertility. Here, as in the Roman world, cats brought good fortune and were associated with good things. Not that this necessarily boded well for the individual cat. Just as in some early cults of the mother goddess, fertility rituals might demand the sacrifice of the king or a virgin, a cat was sometimes demanded as the creature offered up to ensure renewal of the fertility of the earth, a good harvest or blessings of some other kind. However, this did not always mean that the cat had to die. At harvest time in the Dauphine in France the cat was decorated with ribbons and flowers at the beginning of the harvest and if any reapers cut themselves, the cat was made to lick the wound.

It was not only crops that cats would aid. A form of cat sacrifice must

GARRICK THEATRE
LONDON.
Telephone No. Temple Bar 8713.

Commencing Boxing-Day, Dec. 26th.

DICK WHITTINGTON
PANTOMIME

16

be the origin of the cats' bodies found buried in the foundations of buildings or enclosed within a wall. This was still being done in London in the eighteenth century and probably much later. It has been described as a charm to keep mice and rats away – perhaps providing a spectral cat to scare them – but its origins lie in a much wider application of guardianship and good fortune.

The European tradition also included cats which, if you treated them well, would return your favours many times over. These were magician cats or matagots. One of them was linked with the rise of Richard Whittington from poor boy to wealthy merchant and Lord Mayor of London at the end of the fourteenth century. In fact, this was probably as a result of successful trading in coal brought by sea from Northumberland in a vessel called a catboat, but the popular story which later associated his fortune with a domestic cat companion is typical of the belief. Another matagot is featured in the French fairy tale of Puss in Boots - a story which may have its origins a thousand years before its seventeenth-century retelling by Charles Perrault.

The association of cats with the old religions brought them into disfavour with the fathers of the early Christian Church. Often pagan festivals, such as Easter, were adapted and given new meaning as Christian celebrations, and this may have happened with some cat

rituals. Each Corpus Christi at Aix-en-
Provence a cat was wrapped up like a
baby and shown to the congregation
before being burned at midday in a
ceremony. It is difficult to find a
Christian meaning – but the ritual has
clear links with pagan traditions. Even
ceremonies such as that still carried
out each year at Ypres, in Belgium, in
which live cats (these days they are
stuffed cloth substitutes) were thrown
from the belfry of the city hall were
probably originally a celebration of the
cat's magical powers. Nowadays, the
ritual is interpreted as an exorcism of
evil.

Not all churchmen were against
the cat. Cats became associated with
some saints as their companions,
especially with the first-century St.
Martha and second-century St.
Agatha. Under a later thirteenth-
century monastic code the cat was the
only companion permitted to
anchoresses (female hermits). One
notable cat-lover was Pope Gregory
the Great, who took a pet cat with him
as a companion when he retired from
office in 604.

The practical value of the cat was
also becoming more widely
recognized. A ninth-century king of
Saxony set a heavy fine for anyone
who killed an adult cat. A century
later, a Welsh king set values for cats:
a good mouser able to rear her kittens
was valued at four pence. Pet cats
were only worth a penny – unless they
belonged to someone of higher rank. If
they belonged to the king, they were
worth one pound!

But the strength of heretical sects
in the thirteenth century made Church
authorities again turn against the cat.
As one French writer asked: 'Why do
cats sleep or feign sleep all day long,
by the fire in winter or in the sun in
summer?' The answer was not
because, at night, cats were hunting
mice but because they were on watch
in barns and stables to warn evil
spirits if someone was coming so
that the imps and demons could
disappear!

There were rumours that the devil
was worshipped in the form of a huge
black cat – and these suggestions were

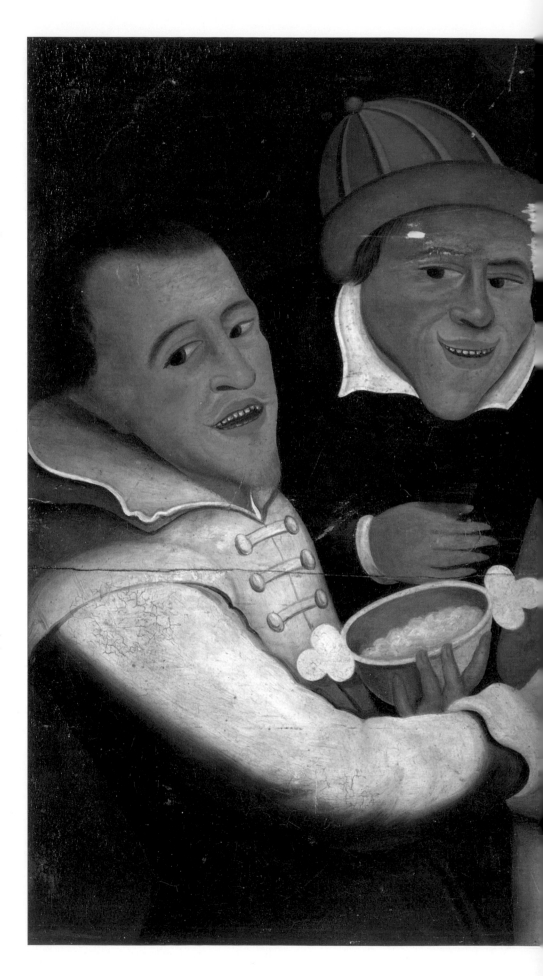

LEFT
An anonymous painting, probably painted in the Netherlands about 1600. The subject has not been identified. Perhaps it illustrates some forgotten Dutch proverb, though it also echoes an ancient custom at Aix-en-Provence, in the south of France, where a cat used to be wrapped like a baby and carried in procession on Corpus Christi Day and, then, according to some accounts, was burned at noon. The people here look too cheerful for them to be tending a sick cat. Since two of the women are holding spoons, are they all taking it in turns to feed the cat from the porringer? The swaddling bands immobilize the cat so that it cannot struggle against these indignities.

ABOVE
Woodcuts
from The History of Richard Whittington, published about 1700. They show Dick as Lord Mayor of London and as a young man offering his cat as his investment in the trading voyage that made his fortune

Puss in Boots *an illustration*
by Gustave Doré (1832-1883).
Here puss stops the Royal coach to con the
king into believing his young 'master' is a
Marquis who has had his clothes stolen
whilst bathing in the river.

knight claimed to have seen in the form of a hissing black cat. Each year, for centuries afterwards, the city burned 13 cats in commemoration.

The cat as a representative of evil and the Devil appears in many paintings, but, by a strange paradox, through its connection with the old virgin and mother goddesses, it also represented the Virgin Mary's divine fertility. It is difficult today to interpret accurately symbols which were probably quite clear to our ancestors. Perhaps the cat sometimes represented both meanings at once, as well as appearing as a natural part of the domestic scene. In other images the cat's good grooming and the care of its appearance have caused it to be used to represent pride. Similarly, probably because of its noisy proclamation of its readiness to mate, it also represented the sin of lust.

Worse was to come. Officially the Church tended to ignore the possible power of witchcraft, but in the thirteenth century its attitude changed. This culminated in a Papal Bull in 1484 that ordered the rooting out of any who cast spells, made charms or 'abandoned themselves to devils'.

The goddess Diana, Roman successor to Bast, was becoming confused with another goddess, Hecate, who was thought of as the Queen of Witches. The cat was naturally linked with her and, whether as a devil or as a servant imp or 'familiar', was again incriminated. Witches were also thought to be able to turn into cats. Folk traditions include many stories of witches surprised and maimed in cat form at night and of women discovered next day bearing the same newly-inflicted injuries.

For centuries those who practised old folk medicines and similar skills were at risk of being accused of witchcraft. Thousands of men and even greater numbers of women were burned, hanged or drowned throughout Europe. Having a pet cat, especially one that was seen on your bed, could strengthen accusations as proof of having a 'familiar' and of having sexual relations with the Devil.

endorsed by the Pope in 1233 and became a major accusation against heretics. In the next century, when the wealthy Order of the Knights Templar was forced out of the Holy Land and moved to France in large numbers, the king felt threatened by their power. He gained Pope Clement V's agreement to their being arraigned on charges of worshipping the big black cat and of unnatural sexual practices. Confessions were gained under torture, and the Order was suppressed. At Metz in 1344 an outbreak of St. Vitus dance was blamed upon the Devil, whom a

LEFT
Adam and Eve (detail)
engraved by Albrecht Dürer (1471-1528).
The artist has symbolically placed a
number of animals in the composition. It
has been suggested that, while those in the
background represent the different
humours of the human temperament, the
mouse personifies the weakness and
vulnerability of man, preyed upon by the
cat, symbolizing evil, which is linked by
its tail to woman, who is already being
tempted by the serpent.

RIGHT
The Annunciation
by Lorenzo Lotto (1480-1556).
Painted about 1527, this picture shows a
rather malicious-looking cat sprinting
away from the angel who brings the news
to the Virgin Mary that she is to be the
mother of Christ. Is the cat a demon
fleeing the messenger of God or just an
ordinary animal frightened by the sudden
arrival of this extraordinary winged
visitor? It is a strange anomaly that
because of its link with the ancient virgin
goddess, the cat can represent the Devil
and the evil from which Mary is free and
from which man will be redeemed by the
death of the Saviour, and at the same time,
the virginity of Mary.

ABOVE
A misericord carving in the Öde Kerk
(Old Church) in Amsterdam. These little
ledges on the underside of seats in the
monastic church were intended to give
some support to tired monks who were not
supposed to sit down during the night-
time offices. They are often carved with
lively scenes. The cat is here linked with a
bat. The two night creatures are probably
intended as a warning of the 'forces of
darkness' against which the monks must
always remain vigilant.

ABOVE
The Last Supper
by Francesco Bassano,
the younger (1549-92).
In their presentations of this subject many
artists, such as Domenico Ghirlandaio,
Tintoretto and Cosimo Rosselli in a
painting of the Last Supper in the Sistine
Chapel, showed a cat near Judas as a
symbol of this treachery, often confronting
a dog as an emblem of faith and fidelity.
Here the symbolism, if intended, is not so
obvious and Francesco, along with his
brothers and his father Jacopo da Ponte,
who was given the name Bassano after the
town where he was born, were among the
first to use animals in natural and
domestic settings of biblical subjects.
What appears to be the same cat can be
seen in a number of their pictures and
must have been their family cat.

RIGHT
The Madonna of the Cat
by Federico Barocci (c. 1535-1612).
Here the cat seems to be part of a
charming domestic scene, but the older
boy (Jesus's cousin St. John the Baptist,
identifiable by his cross nearby) is holding
aloft a goldfinch. This bird likes thistles,
and in Christian iconography is a symbol
of Christ's Passion through His crown of
thorns. (The bird's French name,
chardonerette, *emphasizes the link with*
chardon – thistle.) The cat can, therefore,
be seen as representing evil opposed to
redeeming good.

Witch-mania crossed the Atlantic with colonists to the Americas. One of the best-known instances of this phenomenon occurred at Salem, Massachusetts. In 1692, 150 people were accused of being witches. One man's evidence included a she-devil which 'came in at the Window [in] the likeness of a Cat, which fell upon him, took fast hold of his throat, lay on him a considerable while, and almost killed him'.

The last witchcraft trial in Britain was in 1712. It involved a woman who was said to have been seen conversing with a cat. Though found guilty, she was pardoned. On the European continent trials went on for longer. As late as 1749, a nun in Bavaria was not so lucky. She kept three cats in her room and was made to confess that they talked to her and were really devils. The unfortunate woman was found guilty and beheaded.

25

LEFT
A Halloween card of 1908 repeats the traditional romantic image of the cone-hatted witch riding her broomstick accompanied by her cats, but the image is no more sinister than the pumpkin that forms part of the design.

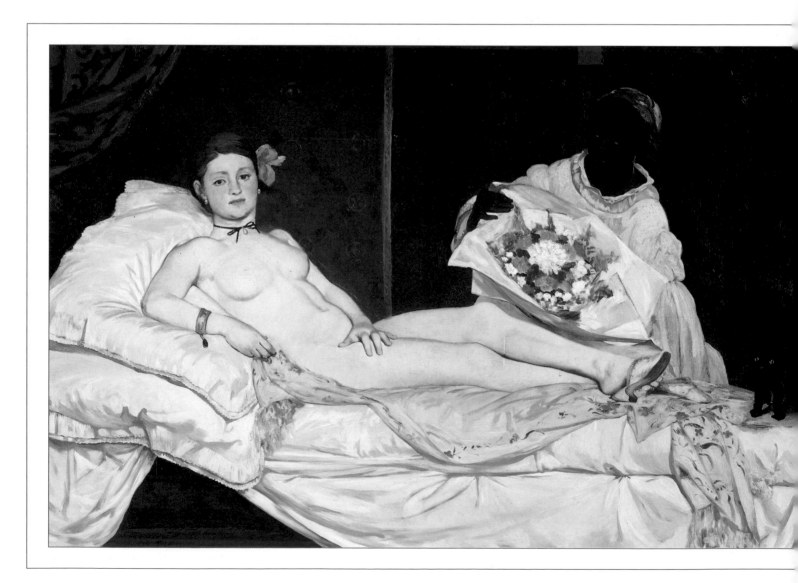

LEFT
Tuesday
by Leonora Carrington (b. 1917).
What roles do the Siamese and tabby cats play in this surreal fantasy, and why does the female who carries them have a second feline head? Here the spectator must try to unravel the artist's personal symbolism for her images do not follow the old iconographic codes.

EFT
Olympia
*by Edouard Manet (1823-83)
was obviously inspired by Titian's* **Venus
of Urbino** *of which he had made a copy
ten years earlier. When first exhibited in
1863 it caused a scandal with its blatant
sexuality. The often noisy call of the
female cat and the noise made by courting
toms draws attention to their mating
behaviour. This may well have been a
major reason for the association of the cat
with lustfulness. It is probably why, at
one time, 'cat' became a synonym for
prostitute and 'cathouse' for a brothel. Is
this the significance of the black cat which
Manet substitutes for Titian's little
spaniel and which is standing, wide awake
and with its tail signalling a greeting,
while Titian's dog is sleeping?*

Next time you call the cat for supper, beware of listeners. Witch-hunting, although in different form, has been known in our own times, too.

Cruelty to the cat did not end with witchcraft trials. Live cats were still used at Ypres until 1817. Sadistic or simply thoughtless people, still subject cats to torment. Popular fiction continues to link the cat with witchcraft and evil in horror movies and stories. Superstitious beliefs persist that the cat can bring both bad and good luck. For most, however, this is a symbolic cat, not a real one. The nineteenth century brought a change of attitude for the real cat. Enthusiasm grew for the cat as domestic pet and it began to be regarded more with cosy sentiment than suspected for its sinister connotations.

A Musical Gathering of Cats
by Ferdinand van Kessel (1648-96).
Did the Dutch artist intend this rather
disquieting picture to be humorous, as the
mouse notation would suggest? It is
apparent that he has not drawn on

observation of real cats, particularly from
the turned-out, backward-pointing ears
that give them all an angry and frightened
look. There are numerous records of
singing cats and cat choirs. Sometimes
they were shut in boxes, their 'voices'

matched to a scale, and their tails pulled to
make them 'sing'; one old print has a devil
pulling their tails. However, some appear
to have been trained to sing without being
cued by pain. One trainer even presented a
'Cats' Opera' in London in 1758.

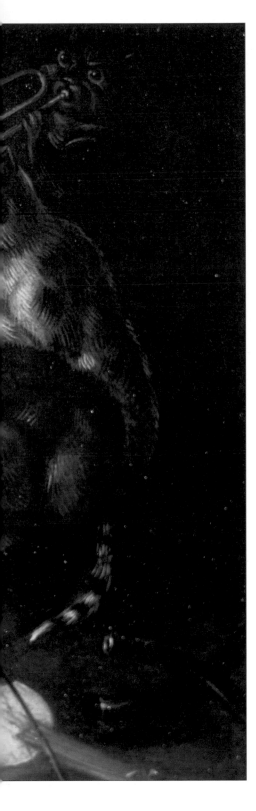

Cat acts appeared with several circuses, and the skills these cats are displaying on a French circus poster of the late nineteenth century suggest that they may have been a famous troupe trained by George Techow. They could safely work with birds and mice, jump through hoops of fire, balance on their front paws and do the complicated routines shown here.

29

The Oriental Cat

The domestic cat spread eastwards from Egypt. Long-haired types, which we now know as Angora and Persian, seem to have developed in the areas now called Turkey and Iran. Islam looked on the cat with kindness. One of Mohammed's disciples was known as the 'Father of Cats' because of his liking for them, and the Prophet himself was said to have once cut off part of his robe rather than wake a cat sleeping on it.

As the domestic cat moved further into Asia, there may have been some interbreeding with native wild forms of the species. As particular blood lines became isolated, this, too, may have promoted the survival of types genetically different from the original

Egyptian. In south-east Asia (although not only there) the pointed pattern of the Siamese appeared, and in Japan the scut-like appendage of the bob-tail was first seen.

It is not known when cats reached China. The first known pictures of

ABOVE, LEFT DETAIL
The Arab Scribe, Cairo
by John Frederick Lewis (1805-76).
The cult of Bast persisted in Egypt until the Roman Emperor Theodosius suppressed paganism in AD 392. Whereas in the Christian Church the threat of re-emergent paganism caused persecution of the cat, in the Middle East the tenets of Islam, established by the Prophet in the early seventh century, looked on cats benevolently.

them there are in portraits of children painted in the Sung Dynasty (960-1279), suggesting that they were then prized pets of the nobility. Stories about cats appeared much earlier in a sixth-century tale of evil spirits used against an Empress, although this does

not prove they were domesticated. There was also a cat fertility god worshipped by some farming communities. In the ninth century a cat from china was presented to the Emperor of Japan. If it was not the first cat in Japan, it was certainly a rarity.

So, too, was another from Korea presented to the Imperial Court a century later. To have been such important presents they were obviously considered special in mainland Asia too.

Although their rodent-catching capabilities were well known, cats were pampered pets. Token cats in painted or ceramic form were set up to scare off mice and rats. The china cats often had a candle placed inside to make them more visible to their potential prey – and they were thought to scare away evil spirits, too. Evil spirits included devil cats. In Japan, as in Europe, witches and cats were thought to be in association. Fortunately, it was easy to recognize some demon cats – they had bifurcated tails. The establishment of the bob-tailed cat in Japan may be partly due to a preference for this stump-tailed variety; it was thought that this sort of tail would not split and grow into two as a normal tail might and, therefore, the cat could not become a demon.

Double-tailed cats appear in both Chinese and Japanese pictures, and a number of artists seem to have been captivated by the cat. The great Japanese cat-lover was the early nineteenth-century artist Kuniyoshi. His studio was home to many pet cats. They not only appear in his pictures as playful pets and as demon spirits, but also as a means of interpreting the different characteristics of way-stations on the Tokaido Road or curled into the positions of Japanese calligraphy.

The most famous of all Japanese cats was one that lived at the Temple of Gotokuji, in what is now part of Tokyo. Known as the Maneki-neko, or 'Beckoning Cat', it sat beside the road outside the temple and beckoned to passers-by to come inside. Its success turned a poor temple into one that became richly endowed. Gotokuji is now a place to which cat-lovers come to ask a favour from heaven for a sick or ailing cat, or for continuing health and happiness. When cats die, people take their ashes there and then return to pray for their cats' spirits.

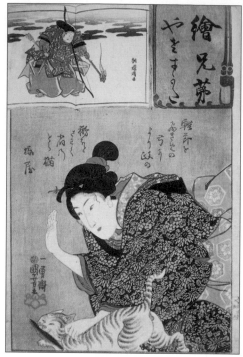

ABOVE
Girl Chastising a Theiving Cat
*a wood block print by Utagawa Kuniyoshi
(1797-1861), an artist who was very fond
of cats which appear in many of his
pictures. Kawanabe Kyosai, who was his
pupil when a little boy, later sketched
Kuniyoshi painting with a cat held in one
arm while other cats wash themselves and
kittens play about his studio.*

LEFT
Cat amidst Flowers
*by Ran'ei, an early nineteenth-century
Japanese artist, painted on silk. What is
the cat watching so intently? Is it one of
the craneflies high above its head? Cats
concentrating on a bird or flying insect
out of reach or beyond a window pane will
often make a machine-gun-like stuttering
noise which seems to express their
annoyance at being frustrated from
catching it?*

The Beckoning Cat itself has become a general lucky symbol, often found in homes or businesses as a talisman to bring prosperity and good fortune. It is found as a talismanic ornament in Japanese houses and sometimes as a welcoming figure near the entrance to shops and restaurants.

A traditional story about a temple cat in Burma tells of the origin of the pattern and colouring of what we now call the Birman. This cat was one of a group of pure white cats living with monks at a temple dedicated to a blue-eyed, golden goddess. This was centuries ago, at a time when an invading army from Thailand was pressing forward, conquering the land. The monks were gathered around their goddess beseeching her protection from the approaching soldiers, when the oldest, senior monk died. As his soul left his body his favourite cat jumped onto his head, and his departing spirit entered the cat's body. As it did so, the cat began to change. Its eyes became the bright shining blue of the goddess's own eyes and its ears and feet took on the dark colour of the earth as a tint spread through its fur, changing it to the soft gold of the goddess's body – all except the paws which retained the pure white of the old monk's hair with

ABOVE
A scene from a Kabuki play based on the story of a witch cat at Okabe, on the Tokaido road, by Utagawa Kuniyoshi. A demon cat dances beside one of the witch's attendants and a huge spectral cat fills the background. There are many Japanese tales of witch cats.

which they were in contact. The cat turned to face the invaders. The monks, amazed and strengthened by this token of the goddess's protection, steeled themselves to defend the temple. Next day, not only was the temple safe, but all the cats had the markings, white paws and blue eyes of the Birman.

This pattern of a dark face mask and lower legs set against a pale coat – though without the white extremities – is also that of the Siamese, one of several cat breeds illustrated on an ancient Siamese scroll. Thai tradition claims that when someone who has reached a high level of enlightenment dies, his soul passes into a cat, remaining there until the cat dies, and then it ascends into heaven or the state of Nirvana. For this reason, a Siamese

BELOW
Tiers of ceramic figures of the Maneki Neko, the 'Beckoning Cat' presented as offerings at the Gotokuji Temple. The Maneki Neko is a talisman for prosperity and good fortune throughout Japan. The original cat has become stylized into a plump white cat wearing a red collar, with black patches on its fur and the insides of its ears red. These figures range from tiny ornaments up to several times life size.

34

cat used to feature in the funeral ceremony of the kings of Thailand. A cat would be placed in the burial chamber at their entombment; when it emerged through a small aperture, deliberately left in the roof for this purpose, it signified to the priests that the transference had occurred. Even in this century, such a cat was carried in the coronation procession of a Thai king so that his predecessor could be present at the crowning of the new monarch.

The first European picture of a cat with Siamese-type markings shows one which German explorer and naturalist Simon Pallas saw in the region of the Caspian Sea in 1794. He reported it as the offspring of a black mother, so it may have been a chance mutation. His engraving looks very different from the cats illustrated in the Cat Book Poems, the Thai picture scroll. It is much darker and heavier than the slim cats of Bangkok, which had dark marks only on ears, tail, muzzle and the lower parts of their legs. However, temperature has an effect on the depth of colour in the coat and the colder Caspian region may account for the darker coat and a heavier layer of fat to keep the cat warm. The scroll paintings may also show young cats – another reason for their having a lighter build and less extensive points.

The Cat Book Poems show other local breeds, as well. These include cats that look like the modern Burmese, and the cat with silver-tipped blue fur now called the Korat. This is known in Thailand as the Si-Sawat – another cat that is said to bring good fortune.

Many fanciful tales have accounted for the crossed eyes and kinked tail which used to be a feature of the Siamese breed. One involved its guarding a goblet, wrapping its tail around the stem. Another described the distortion as resulting from a princess slipping her rings upon it when she went bathing. The cat's eyes became crossed from concentrating for so long on what it was guarding.

Although a Korat appeared at a London cat show in 1896, the breed

did not become established in the West until other examples were taken from Thailand in the 1960s. These became the ancestors of the modern breed. Siamese cats were said to have been introduced with a pair presented to the British Consul, who took them back to England in 1884, although they had been known for some years before then. However, whether the breed originated in Thailand, these particular cats most indubitably did. It is appropriate, too, that the modern Birman breed was apparently founded with two cats that were a gift from priests in a temple in Tibet.

LEFT
A twentieth-century Japanese stoneware figure.

BELOW
The Cat's Voyage
by Ryozo Kohira (b.1947) A contemporary artist working in Europe who has made a number of studies of cats here puts his subjects under the influence of the saki bottle.

The Natural Cat

In the past century, and especially in recent years, cat breeders have produced a number of new breeds and extended the range of coat colours and patterns in existing breeds. Nevertheless and in spite of domestication, the cat's nature has changed little from that of its wild ancestors. It has learned to live with humans and to exploit the facilities they provide. Like most pets when owners maintain a close relationship, it has tended to retain juvenile characteristics. Interaction with its owner may result in elements of the way in which a kitten behaves towards its mother. This is especially likely if the cat is a female or neutered male. Its instincts, however, remain those of the wild animal. In earlier centuries this must have been even truer, not just because of their being that much closer to original domestication, but because, for most cats in most societies, there was little human attention, so human interference was, therefore, much less.

The centuries of association with the gods of Egypt lasted for two thousand years – for as long as Christianity has existed. However, once those days were over, the cat was rarely depicted in its own right. Except for the occasions when it is illustrated in a bestiary, it usually occurs only in symbolic roles or as a minor element in a wide-ranging scene.

As European painting began to deal with incidents from daily life, rather than being restricted to religious subjects and episodes from history and mythology, the cat began to appear in domestic scenes. Often it is taking advantage of the warmth of a hearth, occupying the seat of a chair to keep it above the worst draughts or enjoying the comfort of a cushion. Sometimes it is seen in confrontation with other animals or fighting its own kind. It is frequently discovered as a thief, stealing from the table or the kitchen. It may be shown in patient wait for prey or pouncing on its quarry. Before the nineteenth century the solo portrait of a cat was rare, but sometimes a cat is very realistically portrayed. Sketches left by a number of artists show that they carefully observed the cats they drew. Some artists tried to catch the liveliness and movement of the cat, as well as the contentment of its sleeping form.

The quality of painting and the accuracy of observation offer powerful evidence of the way that each individual artist felt about cats. It is easy to see which painters were working from a hazy memory or a lack of understanding of feline nature when the cat is less satisfactorily portrayed than other parts of a particular scene. There are some painters who have rendered cats with particular skill, and one or two who have become known for their cat pictures.

Leonardo da Vinci's notebooks show him sketching all kinds of things with the same careful observation, so it would be misleading to claim him as a great cat-lover on the basis of a page devoted to cats. In fact, he seems to be in the process of transforming some of them into other creatures. He is not the only one of the great masters to have depicted cats with flair and skill.

A sketch may often capture movement more readily than a painting. The narrative sequences of Théophile Steinlen, although touched

Kitten with Butterfly.
Despite the apparent resemblance of its technique to brushstrokes, this is not a painting but the work of an unknown twentieth-century embroiderer. A fluttering butterfly makes an enticing prey – still when it settles and relatively slow in flight. Cats will sometimes catch them in their mouths or may strike them to the ground with a paw.

活潑玲瓏

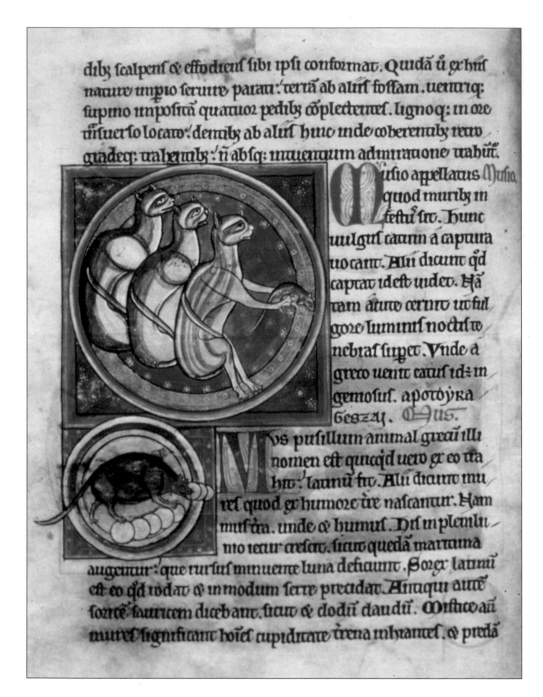

ABOVE
A page from a medieval manuscript
bestiary, including the entries on the cat
and the mouse. These medieval books of
animals are compilations from other
sources, such as Herodotus and Aristotle,
and generally draw heavily on an early
Greek version known as the Physiologus,
dating from the fifth century or earlier.
They repeat unsubstantiated fancies and
include mythological beasts, but the
monks who wrote and copied them knew
cats first-hand so they could at least draw
them reasonably correctly! The Latin
accompanying this reads: 'She is called
Mouser because she is fatal to mice. The
vulgar call her Catus the Cat because she
catches things [a captura], while others
say that it is because she lies in wait
[capat] – she "watches". So sharply does
she glare that her eye penetrates the
shadows of darkness with a gleam of light.
Hence from the Greek comes catus –
"acute".'

ABOVE
Still Life with Cat
by Jean Jovenau (1888-?).
Elegantly arching its back, this cat is
stretching, its tail confidently in the air.
Perhaps it has only just woken up.

BELOW
Cat with a Fish in its Mouth
by an anonymous Indian artist. Painted towards the end of the nineteenth century in the region of Calcutta, this is in the folk-art style known as Kaligat (from the old name for the city), which also produced distinctive simple woodblock prints. The cat has been given human eyes, with coloured irises and visible whites (all of which are coloured in a cat) and this helps produce the anthropomorphic appearance.

with humorous caricature, show a sharp understanding of cat character.

Cats spend much of their lives in sleep and a large proportion in grooming. In the wild, however, their lives depend upon their ability as hunters. They develop great skill in stealthy stalking, making use of cover and camouflage, keeping a low profile to avoid being seen, freezing if their quarry looks towards them and making a rapid advance when it looks away. They have great patience in ambush, waiting beside a rodent hole or by a path regularly used by their prey, ready to pounce at just the right moment.

Physically, cats are well muscled, able to leap both vertically and horizontally for as far as five times their own length, and they land with great accuracy. They can grip with their claws to gain purchase, have an excellent sense of balance and can run at speed. However, they can only keep it up for short distances, because their heart and lungs are comparatively small, so that cats become exhausted quite quickly.

Cats have acute hearing which enables them to pinpoint the location of a mouse rustling in undergrowth or straw. Their eyes are backed by a layer of reflective cells which increases their sensitivity in dim light – producing the 'eye-shine' that can be seen when a cat looks towards a light source in the dark. They have an excellent sense of smell and share with snakes and some other creatures a special scent organ, set above the upper palette. Sometimes you will see a cat, its jaws slightly open and a disdainful expression on its face, drawing air through its mouth and up into this organ to savour a particular smell.

Scent plays an important part in claiming territory. Urine spraying will mark cat ownership and warn others of proprietary rights. Scent glands on the head and tail come into use and leave a message when a cat rubs against an object (or an owner – although it is the cat that marks its ownership!). Scent will tell all the males in an area when a female is in season and ready to mate. At this time, too, the female may employ a loud call, especially raucous in the Siamese, to advertise her availability, while a tom will answer with courtship calls to encourage her to join him.

Cats have a wide vocal range and use it in communication, especially between a mother cat and kittens, but the most obvious messages in cat confrontations are conveyed through body language. Although well equipped with sharp teeth and claws, a cat will generally avoid a fight if it can establish its precedence without one. The arched-back stance of the angry cat is not entirely the result of feline confidence. It is made up rather of the paradox of the rear advancing and the front retreating. The hair

stands away from the body, especially along the tail, making the cat look bigger. (Even humans experience this natural response when their nape hair prickles.) The cat may enlarge its pupils, spit, snarl, and lay back its ears. All these are really defensive reactions, but they may be read as aggression; the more the back of the ear is displayed, the stronger the aggressive element.

By contrast, a confident and happy cat will walk with its tail held up in the air, the tip often slightly curled, its ears pricked and its head held high. It may lie with its vulnerable belly exposed – which some cats like being tickled. But beware, this is also a ploy used by a threatened cat, for it allows it to bring its powerful rear legs into action, slashing with sharp claws.

BELOW
Playing with Mother
by Horatio Henry Couldery (1832-?). Feline motherhood is a full-time job – washing, feeding and washing again, and teaching and training the kittens for their independent lives. It demands considerable tolerance, which this cat's laid-back ears suggest is being strained.

BELOW
The New Arrival
by Horatio Henry Couldery (1832-?). Is the kitten the new arrival, fluffing up his fur in an attempt to make himself more intimidating, or is the bigger cat, perhaps the kittens' father? The nineteenth-

century art critic John Ruskin thought highly of this painter's work. Of a picture of a kitten exhibited in 1875 he wrote 'in its sympathy with kitten nature and its tact and sensitiveness to the finest gradations of kittenly meditation and motion – unsurpassable'.

OVERLEAF
Cat with her Kittens in a Basket
by Samuel de Wilde (1748-1832). Domestic cats will usually have a litter of four to six kittens, although in 1970 one Burmese produced an amazing 19 kittens,

of whom four were stillborn. They suckle almost from birth, each claiming a personal nipple, which cuts down struggles over who sucks when. Eyes open between the fifth and tenth day, but are not fully functional until a week later.

ABOVE
Jealous Animals, *a nineteenth-century painting of the English School. Whoever named this picture surely got it wrong – this friendly pup is just asking the cat to join him in a game.*

LEFT
Reluctant Playmate
by Horatio Henry Couldrey (b.1832)
Kittens investigate something new with caution. A moving animal may stimulate a chase but kittens learn from their mother what is prey and how to kill it efficiently.

RIGHT
The Mischievious Tabbies
by Clemence Nielssen (fl.1879-1911)
Cats and dogs which share a household often become devoted friends, though the cat may often exact the dominant role.

LEFT
Swiss-born artist Théophile Alexandre Steinlen (1859-1923)
published a collection of **Images sans Paroles,** *including this picture story, which capture the essence of feline behaviour, even though they are constructed to make amusing comic strips. (See also the illustration on page 73.)*

RIGHT
The Blockade Runner
by Briton Riviere (1840-1920). Cats will usually avoid a fight unless forced to defend their territory or lives. Able to leap some five times its own length and with claws that gain a purchase on all except the smoothest surfaces, the cat is well equipped to make use of any available escape route. A confrontation from a safe place where it can spit its scorn is a quite different matter. However, this cat does not yet feel secure enough to turn on her persecutors. This is apparent from her appearance. Her body is flattened, which usually makes an escaping (or stalking) cat less visible, her ears are flattened back, so she is still ready to fight, and the tail remains slightly fluffed out.

Studies for the Fifty-three Stages of the Tokaido

by Utagawa Kuniyoshi (1797-1861). These cat sketches, each showing carefully observed behaviour matched to a different posting station on the Tokaido road, show how closely this Japanese artist understood the cats he loved. Most of these studies are self-explanatory, but a few may need explanation. Top row: the third image is a ceramic cat; third row far right, the cat is reacting to the heat of an ember.

A Bit of Cheese

by Henrietta Ronner (1821-1909). Dutch-born Henrietta Ronner (or Ronner-Knipp, as she later signed herself) was widely acclaimed as an animal painter by her contemporaries. Often rather sentimental, as was contemporary taste, her work, nevertheless, shows an accurate observation of cats and cat behaviour. The black and white mother cat, her tail confidently erect, clearly takes no nonsense from the canine members of her household.

LEFT
Puss Napping

a print by George Baxter (1804-67). Baxter invented a new printing process for large-scale reproduction of paintings, which he patented in 1835. It used carefully etched plates with a system of registration points and oil colours mixed to his own recipe, all carefully printed on a hand press. However, he had little business sense and faced stiff competition from cheap, coloured lithographs. Cats are night animals and crepuscular hunters, but pet cats will often adapt their living patterns to match those of their owners. Like us, they have periods of both light and deep sleep, but their senses are never entirely switched off and the scamper of mice is not easily missed by their sensitive ears.

RIGHT
A Cat Attacking Dead Game

by Alexandre-François Desportes (1661-1743). Cats are opportunists and will scavenge food that is readily available rather than exert effort in hunting. Even a well-fed domestic pet will often seem to delight much more in food that it has stolen than in what is provided for it.

BELOW
Dinner Time

by Julius Adam (1826-74). A hierarchy often develops in a permanent group of cats. An older female is usually dominant, taking precedence when she wants to eat, but siblings will often challenge each other over a bone or a titbit.

The Cat Fancy

There have always been some people who, like St. Francis of Assisi, showed concern for animals. Some Eastern religions envisage souls passing through both human and animal incarnations, and their practitioners treat animals well, knowing that one day they might be animals themselves. Buddhism views violence to any creature as harmful to the whole. However, the nineteenth century saw the beginnings of a general change in attitudes to animals. At this time a sense of responsibility, at least towards the domestic animals which human beings exploit, began to be more general in some countries.

Attention was probably first focused mainly upon horses and beasts of burden. In 1822 the Irish-born campaigner Richard Martin, dubbed 'Humanity Martin' by the Prince Regent, managed to get a Bill passed through the British Parliament which became the first legislation 'against the cruel and unjust treatment of animals'. Only two years later the Society for the Prevention of Cruelty to Animals was founded in London. It later gained Queen Victoria as a patron and was awarded the prefix Royal. Similar organizations later appeared around the world.

These developments may have reflected a greater awareness of social responsibility for other people and for our fellow creatures, as well as a realization that a healthy, well-treated horse provides better and longer service. The growing number of middle-class homes, especially in towns, which could afford to keep and cosset family pets probably also influenced the change. It certainly made more people view the cat as more than a sharp-toothed mousetrap.

Exotic animals have always attracted attention, and rulers had long made presents of animals to other royal menageries as part of the currency of diplomacy. New types of cat also excited interest, as when Angora cats were first taken to France in the sixteenth century, and when English Archbishop Laud 'a great lover of Catts' was presented with some 'Cyprus- catts' in Charles I's reign. People of fashion liked to have a cat that looked different from the common types, and by the mid-nineteenth century a variety of distinctly different kinds of cat were being kept as pets.

In 1871 the artist Harrison Weir had the idea of mounting a show in which the different breeds of cat would be exhibited. He was a Fellow of the Horticultural Society, which had for some years held competitive flower shows. He had seen how these had helped to stimulate an interest in horticulture and plant varieties. He saw his cat show as a way of changing public attitudes and increasing popular acceptance of the cat in British homes, of drawing attention to the different breeds and of encouraging sound breeding practices to maintain them or develop new ones.

There were 160 entries for Weir's first show, which was held at the Crystal Palace – Joseph Paxton's huge glass hall, built for the Great Exhibition of 1851, then dismantled and re-erected at Sydenham in south London. The show went off very well and its success led to many other shows in subsequent years and a vogue for pedigree cats. Eventually the National Cat Club was founded in 1887, with Weir as President. Stud books were begun, with careful records kept of each cat's pedigree and formal registration for their kittens. The first American Cat Association was founded in 1899 and others followed around the world.

The National Cat Club's badge was designed by Louis Wain, a British artist whose name became synonymous with cats. He began as a book and magazine illustrator but, especially after he had cats of his own, cats appeared increasingly in his work until he painted almost nothing else. Some of Wain's pictures are natural studies of real cats and show that he knew them well, but the work for which he became enormously popular was totally anthropomorphic. To be more accurate, he often did not so much ascribe human attributes to cats as take human situations and paint people behaving like people but with clothes sprouting cats' heads, legs, tails and fur. For some years he published successful annual albums devoted to humorous pictures of this

Gabrielle Arnault
by Louis Léopold Boilly (1761-1845).
This prolific French painter of portraits and genre scenes fell into disfavour at the time of the Revolution because of the many court scenes he had previously painted. This picture is a portrait of the little daughter of the Secretary of the Académie Française, Vincent Arnault who was the cousin of the painter's second wife. The cat, a typical Angora, is obviously a well-loved pet.

LEFT
Afternoon at Home
by Louis Wain (1860-1939).
Here Wain has made his cats behave like
humans. Although they still have fur,
their postures are human, their paws
apparently have thumbs for gripping and
he has modified their eyes and mouths to
give more human expressions.

ABOVE
The Mewsical Family
by Louis Wain (1860-1939).
At his most anthropomorphic, Wain has
dressed his cats completely but, however
uncatlike the situations and poses,
something feline still persists which may
account for the enthusiasm with which his
work was received and for its continuing
popularity with collectors. Even the
abstract work painted when he was in a
mental hospital still retains something of
the feline face.

kind and also produced a prolific output of pictures made specially for sale as postcards.

Later he suffered from mental illness, becoming increasingly schizophrenic. He continued to paint, but in periods of mental instability his pictures became increasingly psychedelic, although to anyone who knew of his obsession with cats it would usually be possible to see something like a cat's face as the starting point for the patterns that he created.

The survival of paintings and drawings of recognizable breed types provides useful evidence of the existence of particular breeds and of

Harrison Weir with the winner of the First Prize at the Crystal Palace Show – a Persian Kitten

their spread at a particular time. A breed does not necessarily look just as it does today for, as well as developing new types and colours, breeders have continually modified existing breeds in an attempt to reach what they consider the ideal. From Harrison Weir's day, cat clubs and associations have set down official descriptions, or standards, of what a particular breed should be like, and this is what the breeder tries to follow. However, interpreting a standard has often led to concentrating on specific aspects, which have then been taken to

extremes to emphasize a particular characteristic. The Persian cat, for instance, has been bred with an increasingly flattened face – until breeders realized that this could be bad for the cat, creating breathing problems and blocking the tear ducts. In the same way, the Siamese tended to become ever slimmer and more wedge-shaped in the face. Sometimes the standards themselves are changed to avoid characteristics which are considered undesirable, as in the elimination of the kinked tail from the Siamese.

New breeds and colour varieties are still being created and their proliferation has led to the publication of many breed identification books. Some artists made a speciality of breed studies as part of their work. Unfortunately, some such artwork is inaccurate and shows little observation or understanding of cats and cat behaviour, but there are also a number of fine painters who clearly know their cats.

Standards differ a little in detail between the various cat registration bodies. Some refuse to accept colours in a breed that others recognize, or even veto a particular breed altogether – such as the Peke-faced Persian, whose over-flattened face some associations find unacceptable because of the risk of breeding physically unsound animals. Sometimes they will group cats in a different category: in the United States, for instance, some bodies insist on classifying cats of Siamese type with tabby-markings or of certain newer colours as a separate breed called Colorpoint (not to be confused with a British breed called Colourpoint, which is a pointed longhaired cat!).

There are now about 50 different breeds recognized by one or more cat associations. Some may exist in only one colour and pattern, others in as many as 50 different colour and pattern variations. They can be broadly grouped into shorthaired cats, longhaired cats and cats of 'foreign' type (the last being cats like those of oriental origin). Historic accident, coupled with breeders' taste has

resulted in an American Shorthair of slightly different conformation and a more oblong head than the British and European Shorthair. The longhairs belong to two basic types – the svelte Angora and the rounder-, flatter-faced and more heavily built Persian. Then there are the various breeds based on the types already mentioned in the chapter on the Oriental Cat. In addition, there are a number of intermediate types created by cross-breeding between these main forms.

Despite the enormous interest now shown in the pedigree breeds, the vast majority of the world's cats are non-pedigree. They do not owe their genetic mix to any breeder's careful planning but to the random selection of a mate made by the cats themselves. The 'moggie', drawing on a wider pool of genes, may prove a tougher, more disease-resistant cat, and it can often be just as elegant and full of charm. The main difference is that you cannot predict the way a kitten will

Sleepy Cat 29/60   Eileen Mayo

develop or know for certain what kind of kittens a particular cat will have. Some breeds do seem to tend towards a gentler or a more demanding temperament but, whatever their ancestry, all cats potentially have much more in common in their character and behaviour than the differences in their appearance would suggest. The ways in which they behave as pets and react to the humans in their lives may owe as much to the way in which they are treated as to any genetic predisposition. That said, however, a particular line that is reared for several generations in conditions of security and loving care is more likely to be confident with humans than cats which have been exposed to hardship and mistreatment.

RIGHT
Jack Russell and Persian Cat
by F. Rutherford.
This mackerel or Tiger-striped tabby-and-white long-haired Persian cat, with its white ruff, gloves and chin, does not match the official patterns laid down by breed registration bodies but neither do many other attractive cats.

BELOW
Head Study of a Tabby Cat
by Louis Wain (1860-1939).
This English illustrator became devoted to cats and a keen supporter of the National Cat Club. From about 1890 cats appear increasingly frequently in his work. Many of his pictures were commissioned by the publisher Raphael Tuck, who began to issue some of these book illustrations as picture postcards in 1902. This oil painting of 1912 shows Wain's feeling for an actual cat, in contrast to the humorous anthropomorphic work (see page 55) for which he is best known.

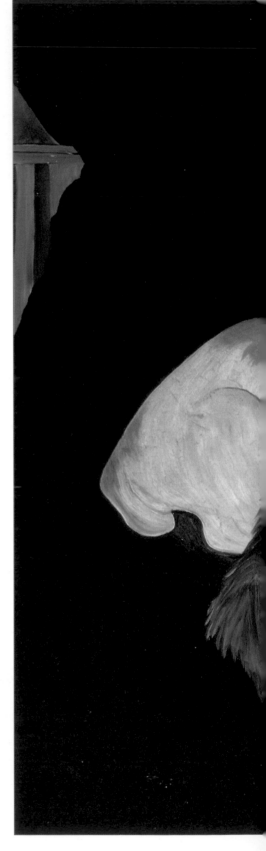

Some rare and recent breeds. Numerous books have been produced describing and illustrating the many breeds of cat. As new varieties are introduced yet further books are needed making demands on artists to show breed characteristics clearly. These studies by illustrator Derick Brown all depict relatively recent and rare types of cat.

The Peke-faced Persian
takes the flattened face of the Persian cat to its extreme. It resembles a Pekingese dog and carries the risk of the same problems of blocked tear ducts and breathing difficulties. As a result, very few cat registration bodies will give it recognition.

The Egyptian Mau
is a return to the cat's beginnings in emulating the spotted cats of ancient Egyptian paintings. It was developed from a pair of cats taken to America from Cairo, although a very similar type was also developed in Europe from the Siamese which retains a Siamese conformation.

The Turkish Van Cat
is an Angora in type and was developed from cats found in the Lake Van district of Turkey, which had the distinctive marking seen here on face and tail. In its native Anatolia, where pure white is considered the proper coat and the colour marking is regarded as an aberration, it is often a keen swimmer.

The American Curl
is a recent mutation that is like an
American Shorthair except for its
distinctively cupped ears.

The Cornish Rex
has curly, wiry hair; its coat lacks the
guard hairs found in most cats' fur. It was
developed from a chance mutation in the
English county of Cornwall. A similar
breed, with some guard hairs that give a
wavy coat, is descended from a cat from
the adjoining county of Devon. It has
much fuller cheeks, prominent whisker
pads and big, low-set ears.

The Sphynx
is a 'hairless' cat, having only an almost
imperceptible down and sometimes a few
hairs on muzzle, legs and scrotum. It
originated in a kitten born in Ontario in
1966. The lack of coat makes this breed
very vulnerable to cold.

Companion Cats

In adressing a poem *'To a Cat'* with the verse quoted on the right Victorian poet Algernon Swinburne is just one poet among many who have written about cats, from the ninth-century Irish monk who penned a poem about his white cat Pangur Ban in the pages of a manuscript he was copying, to the twentieth-century British Poet Laureate, Ted Hughes; from Christopher Smart, writing his wonderful celebration of his cat Jeoffrey while in a home for the insane in the eighteenth century, to French symbolist Charles Baudelaire. Many writers, not just poets, have been drawn to cats, often working with a pet sitting on or by their desks, as Théophile Gautier described the cats of Baudelaire. Gautier himself wrote at length about his own much-loved cats. James Boswell (no cat-lover he) describes lexicographer Samuel Johnson's devotion to them. Colette not only wrote about her cats but, in her performing days appeared on stage as one. That would-be macho representative of the heterosexual male, Ernest Hemingway, surrounded himself with more than 25 cats in his Cuban home, while homosexual aesthete Jean Cocteau was devoted to his Siamese cats.

Novelist William Makepiece Thackeray used to let his favourite cat, Louisa, eat from his own plate. Charles Dicken's daughter described how her father indulged his cat, who, on one occasion, secured attention by using a paw to extinguish the candle by the light of which the famous author was reading, repeating the action when he returned to his book.

Stately, kindly lordly friend
Condescend
Here to sit by me, and turn
Glorious eyes that smile and burn,
Golden eyes, love's lustrous meed,
On the golden page I read.

Another popular nineteenth-century writer, Sir Walter Scott, began by not caring much for cats. His heart was given to his dogs, until a cat called Hinse joined the household, becoming his constant companion. Hinse dominated everyone, including the dogs, for a decade and a half before being killed by a bloodhound who snapped back too vigorously in response to some feline provocation. Mark Twain, too, was a cat-lover, pronouncing quite definitively that 'a home without a cat, and a well-fed, well-petted and properly revered cat, may be a perfect home, perhaps, but how can it prove its title?'

While writers have cherished their own cats, readers have loved the cats they put in their stories, from Beatrix Potter's Tom Kitten to Don Marquis alley queen Mehitabel. There have been talking cats, such as Saki's Tobermory, murderer cats, such as the Siamese in Patricia Highsmith's *Ming's Biggest Prey,* and the numerous cats which T.S. Eliot describes in verse in *Old Possum's Book of Practical Cats,* who were re-created in Andrew Lloyd Webber's musical. There is the foolish Minette and the dashing Briquet in

Honoré de Balzac's *Love Affairs of an English Cat,* the Cheshire Cat in Lewis Carroll's *Alice's Adventures in Wonderland* and Dinah with her two kittens who begin *Alice's Adventures Through the Looking Glass.*

There are a number of cats to be found in the nonsense verse of artist Edward Lear, from the Pussy who sailed off with Owl in their pea-green boat to the Runcible cat. However, none was more important than his real cat Foss, his companion for 17 years, of whom he left numerous sketches in letters. Lear was devoted to Foss and on moving house, when Foss was getting old, he had his new home built exactly like the old one so that Foss would not find it too disturbing.

Lear is known for his bird studies and topographical paintings and sadly does not appear to have painted any cats, but there are many other artists who have been cat-lovers. In the mid-sixteenth century, Jacopo da Ponte of Bassano was one of the first artists to rethink the formal presentation of religious subjects as more natural scenes with rustic settings including ordinary people and animals.

Girl with a Cat
by Pierre August Renoir (1841-1919).
The great French Impressionist included cats in a number of his portraits of attractive women, and in one nude study of a boy. They are always being made a fuss of and surely must have been well-loved pets.

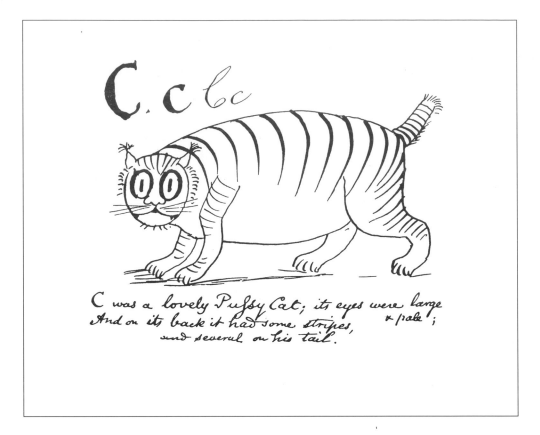

C was a lovely Pufsy Cat; its eyes were large
& pale;
And on its back it had some stripes,
and several on his tail.

In several pictures by him and by other members of his family an identical cat appears; it is tempting to imagine it must have been their own house cat. Although many cats appear in other pictures, it is an engraving by Wenceslaus Hollar of the cat of the Grand Duke of Muscovy that has the first clearly titled identification. However, a portrait of Henry Wriothesley, the young Earl of Southampton who was William Shakespeare's patron and likely

Henry Wriothesley, third Earl of Southampton *(detail)*
by John Critz the Elder (c. 1552-1642). The young earl was imprisoned in the Tower of London (seen in the top corner of the painting) for his involvement in the Earl of Essex's rebellion against Elizabeth I. According to a much later account, his cat found it's way from his home to his prison and down the precise chimney of his room there, to be his companion until his release. The inclusion of the black and white cat in this contemporaneous portrait of Southampton in the Tower seems to give corroboration to the story.

LEFT and ABOVE
The Graham Children *(detail)*
by William Hogarth (1697-1764).
In his social satires Hogarth often uses the behaviour of a cat to point up the message, but here the family cat has been included in the children's group portrait, along with their pet cage bird, perhaps at the youngsters' own request. However, since this bird also happens to be a goldfinch, is Hogarth deliberately recalling the older symbolic use of bird and cat? In the background he includes a clock with the figure of time as a reminder that these children, like the viewer, will grow old. One wonders why the elder girl is holding out a pair of cherries.

Miss Ann White's Kitten
by George Stubbs (1724-1806).
Although Stubbs was a specialist in
animal portraiture, painting many
individual studies of horses and dogs, this
is the only known cat portrait by him,
painted in 1790.

dedicatee of his sonnets, shows a black and white cat beside him which was his prison companion in the Tower of London.

Cats appear often in genre paintings from the eighteenth century onwards, and an increasing number can also be seen in portraits of women and children. The inclusion of a cat does not necessarily mean it was a favourite pet, but many must have been. As for the artists themselves – the illustrations Édouard Manet contributed to *Les Chats* by Champfleury (Jules Houson) in 1870 suggest he must have liked cats; so, too, must Auguste Renoir judging by the number he painted, often echoing the

The Godolphin Arabian
by George Stubbs (1724-1806).
This picture was not painted from life, for this famous horse, which was one of the foundation stallions of the Thoroughbred, died in 1753 and the painting dates from later. However, it records the friendship between the horse and the cat which was its stablemate. When the horse died, the cat at first kept vigil by its body and then hid away in the hayloft where it also died soon after.

sensuality of the women they accompany in his paintings. Gwen John, an English artist, little known in her lifetime when she was overshadowed by her brother Augustus and her lover Auguste Rodin, surrounded herself with cats and painted them many times. Like his predecessor Kuniyoshi, Japanese artist Tsuguhara Fujita, who worked mainly in Paris, was another cat-lover, making numerous portraits of them and sharing a self-portrait with a favourite cat. André Derain made sure that he included Pitou, the family cat, when he painted himself surrounded by his family, including the dog, parrot and a peacock!

Young Woman Holding a Black Cat
*by Gwen John (1879-1939), whose house
and studio were house to many cats and
kittens.*

*A cat figure in Staffordshire 'solid agate'
ware, made c.1745. This type of
earthenware, glazed in an attempt to
suggest natural stone, was made by
several British potteries at this date. Cat
figures, though crudely modelled, seem to
have been popular ornaments.*

Cat and Kittens
*by an anonymous American folk artist,
painted c.1872-83.
Cats make a frequent appearance
accompanying children in the portraits
painted by American travelling limners,
not only as well-loved pets but as an
essential contribution to the composition.
They are also often painted on their own.
To introduce a kitten to a ball of wool is
asking for a tangle, but chasing and
pouncing on a plaything is valuable
practice in the skills a kitten needs to
catch its own supper when it is older.*

'Bloomsbury Group' painters Vanessa Bell and Duncan Grant painted their household cats at Charleston. You can find cats, too, in the works of Pablo Picasso, Fernand Léger, in Marc Chagall's surreal memory paintings, even in the playful pictures of Paul Klee. Franz Marc, Klee's one-time associate in the 'Blue Rider' group of painters, painted a number of pictures of cats which, without any attempt to render naturalistic detail, capture the essential qualities of the cat in postures and attitudes that any cat lover will recognize.

Three lesser painters, who do not often find a place in histories of art, were famous in their own times for their cat pictures. Hungarian born, Swiss artist Gottfried Mind (to whom Chamfleury devoted a chapter in his book on cats), concentrated almost exclusively on painting and drawing cats, earning the nickname 'Der Katzen Raphael' (the 'Raphael of Cats'). His favourite cat, Minette, used to sit near him when he worked and, according to visitors to his studio, he would carry on long conversations with her using both word and gesture.

Later in the nineteenth century, Dutch artist Henriette Ronner-Knip achieved the same acclaim. Her pictures often tell a story, capturing a very feline incident set among the trappings of a prosperous Victorian home. In contrast to her carefully painted detail is the work of her younger contemporary Théophile Steinlen, a Swiss artist who worked mainly in Paris. Many of his drawings and paintings were done for magazines or for use as posters, and his models were as often the alley cats of Montparnasse as well-fed pets. His work included a whole series of *dessins sans paroles* (drawings without words) in which he presents the brief story of an encounter between a cat and a frog, a cat and a ball of wool, and other such scenarios, in a sequence of images that is both amusing and accurate in its observation of cat behaviour.

Even better known than Steinlen's humorous picture stories have been

the numerous cartoon cats that have delighted people all over the world, from George Herriman's Krazy Cat to Jim Davis's Garfield, Felix, Korky and the cats of Bernard Kliban, which show every sign of being inspired by a real cat he knows. Then, in a different vein, there is the much loved work of Ronald Searle, whose wide-ranging satires have included many with feline figures.

While artists and writers have presented their own cats in their work, some cats have gained fame simply by their association with a public figure – Nelson, Margate and Jock, for instance, who were Sir Winston Churchill's cats. Jock used to sit in on Cabinet Meetings when the British Prime Minister led his country during World War II, and often served as a hot-water bottle helping the war-effort by 'saving fuel, power and energy', as Churchill once told an aide. Margate turned up as a stray at Downing Street and Churchill named him after the town where he was addressing a conference. Jock, a present to the leader on his 88th birthday, lived at Chartwell, Churchill's country house. The statesman's will instructed that he be provided with board and lodging and 'comfortable residence' for the rest of his life. Another British 'political' cat was Wilberforce, an animal refuge kitten that held office at Downing Street through the administrations of four prime ministers – until Margaret Thatcher became Prime Minister when it was decided to make him redundant.

LEFT
Woman with Cats
by Janos Vaszary (1867-1939).
This pastel by the Hungarian artist perhaps shows a mother cat's concern that her kittens may be taken away. This is not a recommended way to carry any cat!

May Belfort,
a poster by Henri de Toulouse-Lautrec
(1864-1901).

May was an Irish girl who had sung folk
songs and spirituals in London before
finding work in France. In 1895 she met
the diminutive French artist at a Parisian
cabaret called Les Decadents and began an
association with him. As he worked,
Lautrec could often be heard singing – in
heavily accented English – the song with
which she was especially associated and
which she is depicted performing here:
Daddy wouldn't buy me a bow-wow.
He has shown May singing, 'I've got a
little cat. I'm very fond of that, but I'd
rather have a bow- wow-wow!'

Poster

by Théophile Alexandre Steinlen
(1859-1923) for an exhibition of his work
in 1894. The artist painted easel pictures
of cats, but is much better known for his
Images Sans Paroles (see page 46), his
drawings for books and periodicals and his
50 or so posters which employed cats to
sell commodities ranging from drinking
chocolate, tea and sterilized milk to cafés
and veterinary services. His home was full
of cats and he was devoted to them – and
to his daughter Colette, who sometimes
appears with them in his work.

Three Friends on a Kasai Mat
by contemporary artist Derold Page.
The painter has used a decorative formal
composition and naïve style in this group
portrait, simplifying the tabby's stripes,
by bringing them across its chest, and
employing Dalmatian-like spots, which
would be seen only on a china cat.
However, the detail of the ear tufts,
eyebrows and upper line of the eye in the
seated cats and the pose of the cat
stretched out in front suggest real cats
and that the rounder than usual eyes of
the Siamese are not an error but following
life. These seem to be the artist's friends –
and ours – as well as each other's.

French President Raymond
Poincaré, in office during World War I,
and Léon Blum, Premier before and
after World War II, both had Siamese
cats. Former Premier Clemenceau kept
a Blue Persian at the Elysée Palace.

On the other side of the Atlantic,
Abraham Lincoln adopted three
kittens found half frozen when he was
on a visit to General Grant's camp
during the Civil War. Calvin
Coolidge's cat, Timmie, lived amicably
at the White House with a pet canary
which would settle on him without
coming to harm. At the beginning of
the twentieth century Theodore
Roosevelt had a cat called Slippers,

The Cat,
a lithograph by Tsugouharu Foujita
(1886-1968).
A Japanese artist who settled in Paris in
1913 and, apart from a return to Tokyo
during World War II, lived there for the
rest of his life, Foujita was a member of
the Expressionist group and a friend of
Jean Cocteau. His work combines eastern
and western traits and he is best known
for his nudes and his closely observed cat
studies.

Mr. and Mrs. Clarke and Percy
by David Hockney (b.1937).
A work by one of the most popular and best-known of contemporary artists, this triple portrait of fashion designers Celia Birtwhistle, Ozzie Clarke and their cat at the beginning of the 1970s is a favourite among visitors to London's Tate Gallery. Hockney's working sketches show that he has manipulated and simplified the environment. He has manipulated his title, too – for this cat is not really called Percy. Of course, this doesn't stop the cat from looking splendid and being an essential element of the composition.

76

which used to turn up at official receptions and dinners, while Tom Quartz, another of his cats, named for the Mark Twain cat character, had his biography published. Even he, perhaps, was not so widely known as Socks, the Clinton cat, for White House publicists made sure the whole world knew when this 'First Cat' took up residence.

Whether famous or retiring, pedigree or 'moggie', it is possible, perhaps, to choose a favourite cat from history or books or art, but for most cat owners choosing a personal favourite from their own pets is much more difficult. Each cat has its own good points – and bad ones – its individual charm, its particular tricks and foibles. They all deserve the best care and attention and earn the love they get with the delight they bring into our lives.

RIGHT
A Cat in a Cage
by Gottfried Mindt (1767-1874)
The growing popularity of cats was reflected in the acclaim given to this Swiss painter who was called by his contemporaries 'The Raphael of Cats' Presumably it was cat lovers who gave him this soubriquet for the many cat studies he made, rather than art critics comparing their talents. He was a cat fanatic and most of his work was devoted to them. He used to paint with his own cats all around him, especially his particular favourite, who was called Minette.

BELOW
Together Again
by Ryozo Kohira (b.1947). Another Japanese artist working in Europe who, although by no means specializing in animal studies, has painted a number of pictures of his own Siamese cats: a Seal Point and a Tabby Point. This picture, quite different in style from the one on page 35, was painted by way of affectionate remembrance after one of these siblings had died.

Acknowledgements

All pictures courtesy of The Bridgeman Art
Library, London; except the following which
were supplied by
C.M. Dixon 8,9, 13 right
Dover Books 19 left top and bottom
E.T. Archive 11, 16, 17, 32 right, 57 top and
bottom, 59, 69
The Fortean Picture Library 21 top, 24 bottom
left and right
Museé d'Aquitaine, Bordeaux 14 left
Museé d'Orsay, Paris 26 bottom
National Gallery, London 23
Regency House Publishing 59,60
Oriel Robinson 48
Scala 21 bottom right
Tate Gallery, London 70
Viewpoint Projects 12 bottom, 14 top and
bottom right, 20, 21 bottom left, 24 top, 33 top
and bottom, 35 bottom, 46,56,64 top, 78.
By kind permission of His Grace the Duke of
Buccleuch, from the collection at Broughton
House, Northamptonshire, 64 bottom